From Birth
to Five Years
CHILDREN'S DEVELOPMENTAL
PROGRESS

By the same author:

Spontaneous Play in Early Childhood

From Birth to Five Years

CHILDREN'S DEVELOPMENTAL PROGRESS

MARY D. SHERIDAN OBE, MA, MD, DCH, FFCM

London and New York

First published by the NFER Publishing Company Ltd., 1973
Second Impression 1974
Third and expanded edition 1975
Fourth Impression 1976
Fifth Impression 1977
Sixth Impression 1978
Seventh Impression 1980
Reprinted by The NFER-NELSON Publishing Company Ltd., 1981, 1982, 1983, 1984, 1985, 1986, 1987,
1988 (twice), 1989, 1990, 1991

Reprinted in 1992 (twice), 1993 and 1994 (twice) by Routledge
11 New Fetter Lane, London EC4P 4EE
Simultaneously published in the USA and Canada
by Routledge,
29 West 35th Street, New York, NY 10001

© Mary D. Sheridan 1973, 1975

ISBN 0-415-09114-4

Children's Developmental Progress
is based on *The Developmental Progress*
of Infants and Young Children.
First published by Her Majesty's
Stationery Office 1960
Second Edition 1968
Third Edition 1975

Printed in Hong Kong by Thomas Nelson (HK) Ltd

Illustrations by T.S. Graves

Contents

Introduction

There is general agreement that the younger the age at which children with physical, mental, emotional or social disabilities are discovered and fully assessed, the more hopeful is the prognosis for amelioration or complete rehabilitation. Effective case-finding depends upon the recognition of the earliest signs of deviation from normal development. Hence it is essential that all professional workers who deal with children should be familiar with the accepted 'milestones' (or, as I prefer to call them, 'stepping-stones') of development.

The work epitomized in the accompanying charts has been in progress for more than 35 years and still continues. Originally intended for strictly personal use in connection with inquiries regarding the clinical evaluation of developmental difficulties of vision, hearing and spoken language in young children, my first 'scale' was based on a medley of tests which could be easily applied and which did not necessitate special equipment or purpose-planned rooms. The items were selected from the developmental testing-scales available during the late 1930s and early 1940s, principally those of Gesell (1925 and 1938), Stutsman (1931), Buhler (1935), Doll (1935) and Cattell (1940), for babies under two years of age, and various Binet-type scales for children over two years of age. It soon became obvious, however, that these scales (none of them British) did not agree among themselves, let alone with my own findings. Furthermore, none of them provided the graded tests for visual and auditory acuity required for the paediatric assessment of young handicapped children, nor was it easy to derive from them the means of detecting early signs of disorders of communication, unstable personality and social maladjustment. Their authors were pioneer child psychologists who had been chiefly interested in designing pass/fail scales to establish much-needed norms of intelligence or behaviour in order to calculate a numerical quotient of some kind. On the other hand, my own investigations were mainly concerned with attempting to discover a series of more reliable testing procedures based on developmental principles which would

Origin of the Stycar Schedules

not only assist me in earlier paediatric diagnosis, but also in the clinical management of young handicapped children and in the more helpful guidance of their parents and teachers. It therefore became necessary to evolve a number of new tests and to modify some of the existing ones. This self-imposed task proved much more prolonged, complicated and even controversial than I had anticipated. It has been the main preoccupation of my whole professional life.

Available Psychological Testing Scales

During the past 25 years, much further knowledge concerning developmental processes in young normal and abnormal children has accumulated. Many new psychological testing scales, mainly American, although some have been adapted for English users, are now available. Amongst the most popular are the scales of Wechsler (1949 and 1960) and Bayley (1969). The relevant literature is immense. In this respect, the numerous publications of the Swiss psychologist Jean Piaget have been particularly influential. The paediatrician is referred to his own recent summary (Piaget and Inhelder, 1969). A review of American screening inventories has been provided by Thorpe (1974).

British Psychological Scales

In England Ruth Griffiths (1954) has published a useful ability test standardized on British babies under two years, composed of five sub-scales, which yield a convenient profile. This scale, together with its later extension for young children up to eight years, is now widely used. These or similar psychological scales may be employed whenever it is considered desirable to obtain a detailed assessment of cognitive functioning. Reynell (1969) has designed a valuable language scale for young children with separate tests for comprehension and expression. Francis-Williams (1970) has ably discussed the specific learning difficulties of very young handicapped children.

Paediatric Developmental Tests

All subsequent workers in Europe as well as in America owe an outstanding debt to Arnold Gesell who was both a child psychologist and a paediatrician. The final version of his developmental testing scale was published in 1947. In Britain Illingworth (1953, 1972) has been the chief medical exponent of Gesell's teaching, and has published a standard work on the subject which embodies much new material of his own.

A continuing series of Monographs under the general title of 'Clinics in Developmental Medicine' is published by Spastics International Medical Publications (with William Heinemann). Of particular interest to the clinician is No. 36 entitled *Developmental Screening 0–5 years* by Egan, D. F., Illingworth, R. S., and MacKeith, R. C. (1969) summarizing the recommendations of an interdisciplinary working party. Holt (1965) has discussed the comprehensive assessment of multi-handicapped children. Pollak (1972) has published the results of a study in depth of the developmental status of a multiracial group of three-year-old children examined in their own homes.

Use of the Present Schedules

The charts which follow are not intended to produce a quotient of any sort. I was not concerned with designing a psychological scale of the traditional pass/fail type but with devising a needed paediatric tool. Controlled sampling and statistical evaluation of testing situations and procedures have not been possible. In their present form, all have been applied to several hundred children, and some to many thousands. The tests have been carried out mainly in baby clinics, nurseries, schools and hospital wards where it is seldom possible to apply sustained and complicated procedures which necessitate elaborate equipment or laboratory conditions. Hence, apart from the vision and hearing tests which are standardized for distance and/or duration and which demand a number of special toys, pictures and letter-cards (see footnote), the testing procedures require only a minimum amount of common play material and can be applied in any reasonably-sized, quiet, well-lighted room. They do, however, demand careful interpretation and, to this end, the novice is advised to seek practical guidance from an experienced colleague. They call for a certain natural aptitude, an open mind, an observant eye, an attentive ear and wide experience in the handling of young and difficult children. They also require a considerable amount of practice before their full potentialities become apparent.

In order to elicit as much information as they are capable of producing and to prevent invalid conclusions due to inexpert application or uninformed interpretation, it is important that the medical examiner should personally observe and record the child's behaviour in the various testing situations. The manner of the child's response is usually more illuminating than the mere fact of his ability or inability to comply with the instructions. Although the mother's presence is usually desirable, she must be warned not to participate actively in the proceedings unless her assistance is requested. Her report of the child's behaviour in everyday situations should always be treated with respect and carefully recorded, particularly if she voices any anxiety or suspicion that his reactions are abnormal, but in order to prevent any future misunderstanding, the fact that this is hearsay evidence and not personal observation should always be noted in the report. This particularly applies to the recording of spoken language and personal relationships.

The items are arranged in four main sections which reflect the four outstanding human biological achievements, i.e. upright locomotion, hand-eye coordination, use of spoken language and the evolution of complex social cultures (pages 12 and 13). Hence the relevant sections are headed: 1. Posture and Large Movements; 2. Vision and Fine Movements; 3. Hearing and Speech; 4. Social Behaviour and Play. Each of these sections, however, must be sub-divided for the purpose of clinical testing, for instance with regard to the second section, manipulations and visual competence in far and near use must be investigated, and to the third section, auditory competence determined as well as use of language codes. In the assessment of social behaviour, it is necessary to seek evidence not only regarding capability in self-care (dressing, feeding, toilet, etc.) but also regarding the child's ability to establish good personal relationships, his general understanding of everyday situations and his willingness to conform to reasonable social demands.

Recording of Results

It need hardly be said that the usual detailed history-taking and full clinical paediatric examination should accompany the application of these developmental tests. The experienced medical examiner will appreciate that every child presents his own individual challenge and that certain modifying factors must always be taken into account in reaching a clinical diagnosis. For instance, with babies, allowance needs to be made for premature birth, recent illness, hunger, thirst, fatigue or pain, and with older infants and children for distractibility due to excitement, for timidity or anxiety, for grief following separation from family and home, also for the nature of the child's social environment and his opportunities to learn from experience. The words 'pass' and 'fail' are therefore inappropriate. The child is judged to respond or not to respond to each testing procedure in the manner which, in the clinician's opinion, might reasonably be considered satisfactory for an ordinary healthy and contented child of his chronological age. Few children will respond unequivocally to every item listed during a single examination, and many who subsequently prove to have average ability will respond at earlier or later ages than those indicated. There are also innumerable transitional responses which, although too varied and subtle to include in the tables, are nevertheless most revealing in the actual clinical situation. A useful working rule is to expect a positive response to approximately three-quarters of the items listed in each of the four separate sections for children in his key age group. This result may be considered to indicate average functioning in these particular abilities and in the child's general understanding of what is happening in the world around him (rated B). If the child also responds to a quarter or more of the testing situations for the next older key age, his performance may be recorded as 'above-average' (rated A). If he responds only to the procedures listed for the next younger key age and to less than half of the items for his own age group, he may be recorded as 'below-average' (C). With handicapped children in the relevant developmental parameter, a more detailed descriptive record is desirable of the items applied, the manner of response and the levels of attainment achieved. With increasing experience, the examiner may prefer to record his findings on a five-point scale or to construct some form of 'profile' for future reference. (I am presently piloting a form.)

It is important to remember that even the most sensitive testing scales provide evidence of a child's condition on the day of examination only, and that multiple handicaps are the rule rather than the exception. Although unmistakable evidence of motor disability, deafness, or mental retardation may demand immediate referral for the appropriate specialist opinion or treatment, a firm diagnosis regarding the presence or absence of some less obvious additional handicap can never safely be made on the basis of a single examination. Repeated at regular intervals, the tests do provide a useful means of assessing and recording developmental progress and they also offer prognostic indications. Nevertheless, even the results of serial examinations of infants and young children must always be treated with caution. It is unsafe to regard these or any other tests as capable of reliably predicting the ultimate physical or intellectual status of handicapped or disadvantaged children.

Within these limitations this book offers to paediatric practitioners and others concerned, in plain words and tabulated form, information derived from many years' experience with normal and handicapped young children. I hope they may find it helpful in observing and enjoying the developmental progress of normal children, in detecting the earliest signs of physical disability, mental retardation, personality disorder and social maladjustment, and finally in giving sympathetic guidance to parents and others concerned with the treatment, care and training of young handicapped children in the community.

Acknowledgements

The original version of these Stycar Developmental
Sequences entitled *The Developmental Progress of Infants
and Young Children*, was first published in 1960 by HMSO on
behalf of the Ministry of Health (now the Department of
Health and Social Security) as number 102 in the series
'Reports on Public Health and Medical Subjects'. Second
and third editions were published in 1968 and 1975. The
present book is published with the approval of HMSO.

The original text has been completely revised and consider-
ably extended to conform with my recent and continuing
investigations. The drawings were prepared by Mr Tom
Graves from my personal collection of colour slides. The
majority of the original photographs were taken, in their
own surgery, by Dr John Graves, while Dr Valerie Graves
applied the testing procedures under my guidance. Children
were selected by Dr Valerie Graves, who was their family
doctor, as being of precisely the 'key-age' under study, the
parents and children giving their help voluntarily. The
remaining pictures were taken with the assistance of Dr
Pamela Zinkin and Dr Kulsum Winship and many other
colleagues, too numerous to mention, at the Wolfson Centre
of the Institute of Child Health, the Newcomen Centre at
Guy's Hospital, the Nuffield Hearing and Speech Centre at
The Royal National Throat Nose and Ear Hospital, or in
the children's own homes. My sincere gratitude is due to all
these colleagues and to the many hundreds of children who
have so enthusiastically aided me in my investigations over
the years, and to their parents, nurses and teachers.

References

Bayley, Nancy (1969). *Bayley Scales of Infant Development*. New York: Psychological Corporation.

Buhler, C., and Hetzer, H. (1935). *Testing Children's Development from Birth to School Age*. London: Allen & Unwin.

Cattell, P. (1940). *Measurement of Intelligence of Infants and Young Children*. New York: Psychological Corporation.

Clinics in Developmental Medicine. (Specialist Monographs Series). Spastics International Medical Publications. London: Heinemann Medical Books. (Various titles.)

Doll, E. (1935). Article in *Amer. J. Orthopsychiatry*, V, 1.

Egan, D. F., Illingworth, R. S. and MacKeith, R. C. (1969). *Developmental Screening 0–5 Years*. Spastics International Medical Publications. London: Heinemann Medical Books.

Francis-Williams, J. (1974). *Children with Specific Learning Difficulties*. (2nd Edit.) Oxford: Pergamon Press.

Gesell, A. (1925). *Mental Growth of the Pre-School Child*. New York: Macmillan.

Gesell, A. (1938). *Psychology of Early Growth*. New York: Macmillan.

Gesell, A. and Armatruda, C. S. (1947). *Developmental Diagnosis*. New York and London: Hoeber.

Griffiths, R. (1954). *The Abilities of Babies*. London: Univ. of London Press.

Griffiths, R. (1971). *The Abilities of Young Children*. London: Privately printed.

Holt, K. S. (1965). *The Assessment of Cerebral Palsy, Vol. I*. London: Lloyd Luke.

Holt, K. S. and Reynell, J. K. (1967). *The Assessment of Cerebral Palsy, Vol. II*. London: Lloyd Luke.

Illingworth, R. S. (1953). *The Normal Child*. London: Churchill.

Illingworth, R. S. (1972). *The Development of Infants and Young Children: Normal and Abnormal*. (5th Edit.). Edinburgh: Livingstone.

Piaget, J. and Inhelder, B. (1969). *The Psychology of the Child*. London: Routledge.

Pollak, M. (1972). *Today's Three-Year-Olds in London*. Spastics International Medical Publications. London.

Reynell, J. (1969). *Reynell Developmental Language Scales*. Windsor, UK : NFER-NELSON.

Sheridan, M. D. (1958). Article in *Brit. Med. J.*, ii, p. 999.

Sheridan, M. D. (1960). Article in *Brit. Med. J.*, ii, p. 453.

Sheridan, M. D. (1968). *Manuals of Instruction for Stycar Tests of Vision, Hearing, and (1975) Language*. Windsor, UK : NFER-NELSON.

Stutsman, R. (1931). *Mental Measurement of Pre-School Children.* New York: World Book Co.

Terman, L. M. and Merrill, M. A. (1961). *Manual for Stanford-Binet Intelligence Scale.* 3rd Revision, Form L-M. London: Harrap.

Thorpe, H. S. and Werner, E. E. (1974). 'Developmental screening of pre-school children', *Pediatrics, 53,* 3, 362.

Wechsler, D. (1949). *Wechsler Intelligence Scale for Children* (Manual) (WISC). New York: Psychological Corporation.

Wechsler, D. (1960). *Wechsler Pre-School and Primary Scale of Intelligence* (WPPSI). New York: Psychological Corporation. (English versions from NFER-NELSON, Windsor.)

Addresses

The Sheridan Stycar Vision and Hearing Test (Materials and manuals of instruction: copyright) and screening chart are obtainable from

> NFER-NELSON Publishing Company Ltd.,
> Darville House,
> 2 Oxford Road East,
> Windsor, Berks. SL4 1DF

Audio-taped lectures (playing time 35–40 minutes) with 48–64 colour slides illustrating examinations and behaviour of infants and young children from one month to five years are available (speaker Mary Sheridan) for sale or hire from

> Drs John and Valerie Graves,
> MRSF,
> Kitts Croft,
> Writtle,
> Chelmsford, CM1 3EH, Essex.

Seven films on Child Development, designed in collaboration with Dr Neil O'Doherty, are available for sale or hire from

> Robin Franklin,
> Guild Sound and Vision Ltd.,
> Woodston House, Oundle Road,
> Peterborough, PE2 9P2.

The Handicapped Child and his Home by M. D. Sheridan (2nd Ed. 1973). This essay on community care is published by

> The National Children's Home,
> 85 Highbury Park,
> London, N5 1VD

Definitions Relating to Developmental Paediatrics

This is concerned with the health and wellbeing of all children in the community. Its organization and practice demands an adequate supply of community child health doctors, family doctors and consultant paediatricians suitably experienced in the care and management of normal and abnormal children, well or sick, in hospital, at home or in school.

Community Paediatrics

All children, normal and abnormal, progressing from the helplessness of infancy to the independence of maturity, have certain physical needs, without which life itself cannot continue, and certain psychological needs, without which an individual cannot attain contentment, self-reliance and good relationships with other people.

Basic Needs

There can be little disagreement about these seven essentials for existence:
    shelter and protective care;
    food;
    warmth and clothing;
    fresh air and sunlight;
    activity and rest;
    prevention of illness and injury;
    training in habits and skills necessary for the
        maintenance of life.

Basic Physical Needs

These relate both to intellectual and emotional development because these are so closely interwoven that it is difficult to provide for them adequately except in combination. They include:
    affection and continuity of individual care;
    security rooted in a knowledge of belonging, in stable personal relationships and in familiar environmental conditions;
    a sense of personal identity, dignity as a human being, and self-respect derived from knowledge of being valued as an individual;
    opportunity to learn from experience;

Basic Psychological Needs

opportunity to achieve success in some field of endeavour, however small;

opportunity to achieve independence, personal and, so far as possible, financial;

opportunity to take responsibility, however slight, and to be of service to others.

Developmental Paediatrics

This branch of the art and science of paediatrics includes numerous clinical as well as social factors. It is concerned with maturational processes (from foetal viability to full growth), in structure and in function, of normal and abnormal children, for three purposes; *first* to promote optimal physical and mental health for all children; *second* to ensure early diagnosis and effective treatment of handicapping conditions of body, mind and personality; and *third* to discover the cause and means of preventing such handicapping conditions.

Growth and Development

These are not identical.

Growth is increase in size. Its progressions are mainly structural and can be measured with some degree of reliability in terms of height, weight, bone-age, etc.

Development is increase in complexity. It involves both structure and function. Its numerous simultaneous progressions are closely related but manifest many individual variations.

Normally growth and development of body, intellect and personality progress harmoniously and with relative predictability in rate and outcome.

Abnormally, they are dissociated, producing widespread inconsistencies of and between somatic, cognitive and affective progressions, with unpredictable final results.

Biological Characteristics

The four outstanding biological achievements of *homo sapiens* which mark his superiority over all other animals are:

first his upright posture, which facilitates locomotion and enables him to assume, adapt and maintain an enormous variety of effective attitudes while leaving his hands free for more precise activities;

second his finely adjustable visual equipment and uniquely flexible digits which bestow the ability to construct and use hand tools;

third his possession of spoken language;

fourth his evolution of complex social cultures for the benefit of the groups and individuals comprising them, and for protection of the young during their relatively prolonged period of dependency.

The four corresponding parameters of human development are:

Motor, involving body postures and large movements which combine high physical competence with economy of effort.

Vision and fine movements, involving visual competence in seeing and looking (far and near) and manipulative skills.

Hearing and speech, involving auditory competence in hearing and listening, and in the use of speech and language codes.

Social behaviour and spontaneous play, involving competence in organization of the self, i.e. self-identity, self-care and progressively effectual self-occupation; together with increasing voluntary acceptance of satisfactory social standards with regard to personal relationships and cultural demands.

Parallels of Development

In common with all other living creatures man is subject from the moment of his conception to the compelling, inseparable influences of heredity and environment.

Heredity determines the limits of each individual child's capacity to achieve optimal structural and functional maturity.

Environment determines the extent to which each individual child can fulfil his potential capacity.

It is in the nature of the developing *body* to be continually active, of the developing *mind* to be intensely curious and of the developing *personality* to seek good relationships with other people.

Any inactive, incurious or unforthcoming child is in need of full physical and mental assessment and ongoing supervision to ensure that he is not sick, or suffering from an undiagnosed handicapping condition or environmental deprivation, or defending himself against some intolerable stress.

Nature and Nurture

Handicapped and Disadvantaged Children	In one sense, all handicapped children, however well provided otherwise, are disadvantaged and deprived in some way, and all disadvantaged and deprived children are handicapped socially if not physically and intellectually. Broadly speaking, the disabilities of the handicapped child are the result of some pathological condition within himself (endogenous), while the disabilities of disadvantaged and deprived children are the result of unfavourable conditions within the environment (exogenous). *A handicapped child* is one who suffers from any continuing disability of body, intellect or personality which is likely to interfere with his normal growth and development or capacity to learn. *A disadvantaged child* is one who suffers from a continuing inadequacy of material, affectional, educational or social provisions, or who is subject to detrimental environmental stresses of any kind, which are likely to interfere with the growth and development of his body, intellect or personality and thus prevent him from achieving his inherent potential.
Community Provisions for Handicapped Children	In this country, handicapped children have the same right as other children to be cared for, medically treated and educated in accordance with their age, aptitude and ability. If they are to receive the full benefits of citizenship, however, the community must ensure them a number of additional provisions. These include: Early identification; Full assessment of disabilities and assets; Prompt medical and surgical treatment; Help and guidance for the parents to enable them to care for their handicapped child as long as possible in his own home; Appropriate training, education and vocational guidance; Supervision and regular assessment throughout childhood and adolescence; Final placement in the community or in special care.
Early Identification of Handicapped Children	The word 'identification' is preferable in this context because it implies the deliberate seeking out, not only of handicapped children, but of children at risk, whereas the word 'diagnosis' carries too narrow a connotation implying

that the deviating child has already been recognized and referred for treatment.

It is generally agreed that certain groups of children are more likely to suffer from handicapping conditions than the majority of their age group and that these vulnerable infants should be carefully followed up until it is certain whether or not they are able to see, hear, walk, play and communicate normally.

Children at Risk

Infants at risk may be divided into five groups. Children in the first four of these groups present congenital malformations or have discouraging medical or social histories. Children in the fifth group appear to be normal at first, but manifest unfavourable signs or symptoms later. The five groups may be conveniently designated as follows:

Group 1: Adverse family history
Group 2: Prenatal hazards
Group 3: Perinatal dangers
Group 4: Postnatal mishaps
Group 5: Developmental warning signals.

These may be divided into three main categories:

Handicapping Conditions in Children

those which are obvious from birth, e.g. gross congenital deformities, Down's syndrome, etc.;

those which must be deliberately sought for, e.g. metabolic disorders, congenital dislocation of hip, blindness, deafness etc.;

those which only become apparent during the course of development, e.g. cerebral palsy, mental retardation, emotional difficulties, squint, visual and auditory impairments, specific learning and language disorders etc.

Hence the need for reliable developmental diagnostic testing procedures. These fall into two broad categories—those which are designed for *screening* large populations, and those which are intended for more precise *individual* application. Screening tests are valuable only if they can be relied on to identify all the children needing further investigation, without at the same time including too many 'false-positives'.

Screening devices must be simple in application but sensitive in result. Ideally they should be applied to the entire infant population. In practice, owing to limited resources, it may

Diagnostic Procedures

be necessary to focus attention on children in specially vulnerable groups.

Individual investigations are essential in every known or suspected case of handicap. They usually necessitate full clinical and laboratory facilities. They frequently require opportunity for prolonged observation. They sometimes depend upon response to empirical therapies.

Follow-up arrangements: Paediatric supervision should continue until the child demonstrates that he is able to see, hear, walk, talk and play satisfactorily and conform acceptably to social demands.

Developmental Warning Signals

The earliest indications of deviant development usually depend upon:

Mother's suspicions that her child is not seeing, hearing, moving his limbs or taking notice like other children of his age.

NB: She is usually right.

Paediatric findings such as delayed motor development, lack of normal visual alertness, inattention to sound, delayed development of vocalization or speech, lack of interest in people or playthings and abnormal social behaviour of any sort.

NB: It is not safe to rely upon a single examination.

Full Assessment

Comprehensive assessment of a handicapped child must always include his sensory functioning as well as his motor and neurological capabilities, his intellectual competence and his social behaviour. For this reason the traditional psychological child development scales, designed to provide intelligence or social quotients, useful though they are within their own particular terms of reference, must always be supplemented by full paediatric examination, including careful evaluation of the child's visual and auditory capacity and his powers of communication. It is equally important to assess and record the handicapped child's *abilities* and to 'treat' (i.e. train) these appropriately in parallel with the medical and surgical treatment of his disabilities.

Medical Treatment

Provisions for every sort of medical care have always been available to handicapped children under the NHS. In order to ensure the success of any therapeutic programme, however, it is important that full consultation and exchange of relevant information between all the professional people concerned are maintained.

Guidance regarding the care and upbringing of children to ensure their optimum physical and mental health is required by all young parents. Parents of handicapped children need additional case-work support with knowledgeable instruction concerning everyday management. Their needs may be summarized as follows:

Parent Guidance

truthful explanation of the handicapping condition, its causation and prognosis;
continuing supportive counselling for all the family;
practical instruction in day-to-day care and management;
referral to the appropriate social agencies including provision of domestic help and financial assistance;
realistic forward planning;
genetic advice when necessary.

Early training depends upon adequate stimulation. The natural *teachers* are the parents. The natural *place* is the ordinary family home. The natural *tools* of learning are playthings.

Opportunity to Learn

Special education is an integral part of the handicapped child's treatment. His schooling must always be of prime consideration in planning necessary medical and surgical procedures.

Vocational guidance must be based on realistic evaluation of his physical capacity, mental ability and social competence.

It is necessary for all concerned with the health, education and welfare of handicapped children to bear constantly in mind that childhood itself is a temporary phase in the life of any individual human being. The ultimate goal is to equip him or her in body, mind and personality to become in adult life, a contented, self-reliant and useful member of the social community to which he or she belongs.

Ultimate Aims

(Based on a shorter paper originally published in *Health Trends*, August 1969, HMSO).

Illustrated Charts of Children's Developmental Progress

One Month to Five Years

The Normal Neonate

It is not intended to discuss testing procedures for neurological or other assessment of the newborn. The subject has a very large literature of its own. These notes and illustrations are intended only to provide a baseline for comparison with the later progressions particularized in the following sections. It needs to be kept in mind that the reactions of any newborn baby, although mainly reflex in nature, are closely dependent not only upon the baby's maturity and physical condition, but also upon his state of alertness or drowsiness, hunger or satiation at the time of examination.

Posture and Large Movements

Held in ventral suspension (drawing 1) the head droops below the plane of the body, the hips are fully flexed and the limbs hang downwards. Placed in prone, the baby promptly turns his head sideways, his cheek resting on the table top. The buttocks are humped up, with the knees flexed under the abdomen. The arms are close to the chest with the elbows fully flexed.

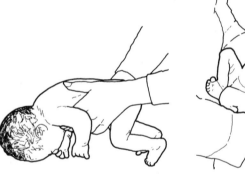

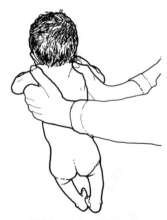

1. Ventral suspension   *2. Moro reflex*

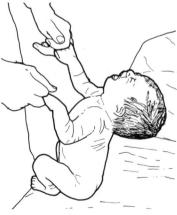

3. Pulled to sitting   *4. Held upright under arms*

The Moro reflex is symmetrical and readily obtained in response to appropriate stimulus. Drawing 2 shows usual method of elicitation, by sudden slight dropping of examiner's hand supporting head.

Pulled-to-sitting (drawing 3) marked head lag is present.

Held in upright suspension (drawing 4) under arms the muscles of shoulders and upper arms demonstrate good tone and power by 'holding' symmetrically for several seconds before gradually 'giving way'. (The quality of 'tone' elicited in this manoeuvre is very obvious in the clinical situation to any experienced examiner).

'Placing' reactions, primary walking, and extension of legs to pressure on soles of feet, are readily demonstrated.

Palmar and plantar grasp reflexes are present.

Rooting, sucking, swallowing and eliminating reflexes present.

Other Manifestations

Pupils react to light (from birth).

Optical closure to sudden bright light (from birth).

'Doll's eye' reflex (first few days).

Turning towards diffuse light (from first week).

Opens eyes when held upright.

Blinks eyes or opens widely to sudden sound.

May 'corner' eyes towards nearby source of continued sound, e.g. voiced 'ah-ah'.

Startle reaction to sudden loud sounds.

'Freezing' reaction to weaker, more continuous sounds.

Cries are vigorous but variable in pitch, quality and duration. These usually cease to nearby, continuous, moderately loud vocalization of adult.

Eyes and Ears

Almost continual drowsiness of first few days gradually gives way to longer periods of alert wakefulness and physical activity. Mothers consistently report that babies manifest numerous subtle indications of individuality from birth. These individual characteristics become increasingly pronounced throughout the whole period under review, and should be carefully recorded.

General

Age 1 Month

Posture and Large
Movements

In supine, lies with head to one side; arm and leg on face side outstretched, or both arms flexed; knees apart, soles of feet turned inwards.

Large jerky movements of limbs, arms more active than legs.

At rest, hands closed and thumb turned in.

Fingers and toes fan out during extensor movements of limbs.

When cheek touched at corner of mouth, turns to same side in attempt to suck finger.

When ear gently rubbed, turns head away.

When lifted from cot, head falls loosely unless supported.

Pulled to sit, head lags until body vertical when head is held momentarily erect before falling forwards.

Held sitting, back is one complete curve.

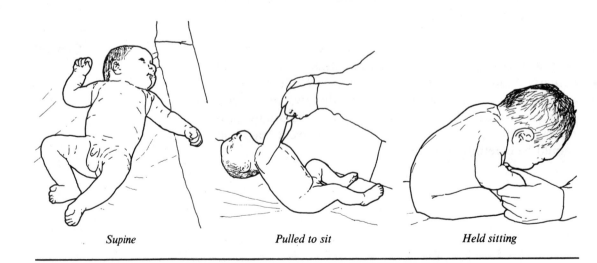

Supine   *Pulled to sit*   *Held sitting*

In ventral suspension, head in line with body and hips semi-extended.

Placed in prone, head immediately turns to side; arms and legs flexed, elbows away from body, buttocks moderately high.

Held standing on hard surface, presses down feet, straightens body and (usually) makes a forward reflex 'walking' movement.

Stimulation of dorsum of foot against table edge produces 'stepping up over curb'.

Age 1 Month

Ventral suspension

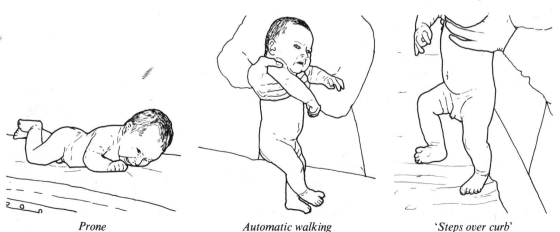

Prone   *Automatic walking*   *'Steps over curb'*

Age 1 Month

Vision and
Fine Movements

Pupils react to light.

Turns head and eyes towards light source.

Stares prolongedly at diffuse brightness of window or lightly-coloured blank wall.

Follows pencil flash-lamp briefly with eyes at one foot distance.

Shuts eyes tightly when pencil light shone directly into them.

Gaze caught and held by dangling (golf-)ball gently agitated in line of vision at 6 to 10 inches towards and away from face.

Follows ball's slow movements with eyes from side towards midline horizontally with face through quarter circle or more, before head falls back to side.

Watches mother's nearby face when she feeds or talks to him with increasingly alert facial expression (from about three weeks).

Defensive blink present by six to eight weeks.

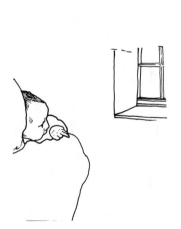

Turns to diffuse light

Eyes follow moving ball

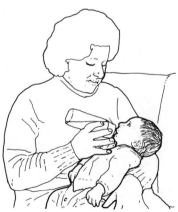

Regards mother's face intently while feeding

Startled by sudden noises, stiffens, quivers, blinks, screws up eyes, extends limbs, fans out fingers and toes and may cry.

Movements momentarily 'frozen' when small bell rung gently three to five inches from ear for three to five seconds with five-second pauses; may move eyes and head towards sound source.

Stops whimpering: and (usually) turns towards sound of nearby soothing human voice, but not when screaming or feeding.

Cries lustily when hungry or uncomfortable.

Utters little guttural noises when content. Coos responsively to mother's talk from about five to six weeks.
(*Note*: Deaf babies also cry and vocalize in this reflex fashion but when very deaf do not usually show startle reflex to sudden noise. Blind babies may also move eyes towards a sound-making instrument. Visual following and auditory response must therefore always be tested separately).

Sucks well.

Sleeps most of the time when not being fed or handled.

Expression still vague but becoming more alert later, progressing to social smile and responsive vocalizations at about five to six weeks.

Hands normally closed, but if opened grasps finger when palm is touched.

Stops crying when picked up and spoken to.

Turns to regard nearby speaker's face.

Mother supports head when carrying, dressing and bathing.

Passive acceptance of bath and dressing routines gradually giving way to incipient awareness and response.

Age 1 Month

Hearing and Speech

Social Behaviour
and Play

Stops whimpering to listen, turns head.　　　*Grasps finger*

Age 3 Months

Posture and
Large Movements

In supine, prefers to lie with head in midline.

Limbs more pliable, movements smoother and more continuous.

Waves arms symmetrically. Hands loosely open.

Brings hands together from sides into midline over chest or chin.

Kicks vigorously, legs alternating or occasionally together.

Pulled to sit, little or no head lag.

Held sitting, back is straight except in lumbar region.

Head held erect and steady for several seconds before bobbing forwards.

In ventral suspension, head held well above line of body, hips and shoulders extended.

Placed in prone, lifts head and upper chest well up in midline, using forearms to support and (often) actively scratching at table surface with hands, buttocks flat.

Held standing with feet on hard surface, sags at knees.

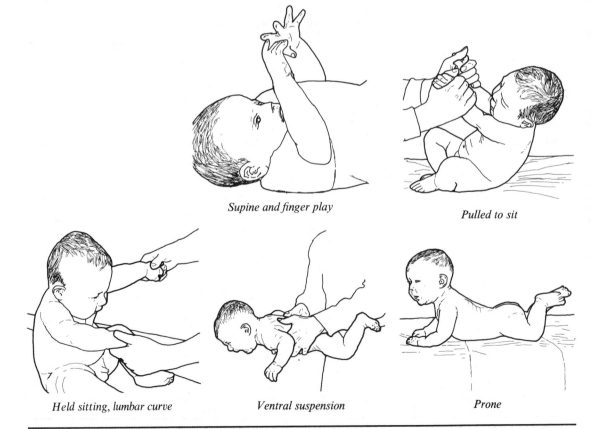

Supine and finger play

Pulled to sit

Held sitting, lumbar curve

Ventral suspension

Prone

Visually very alert, particularly preoccupied by nearby human face.

Moves head deliberately to gaze attentively around him.

Follows adult's movements within available visual field.

Follows dangling ball at 6 to 12 inches from face through half circle horizontally from side to side and usually also vertically from chest to brow.

Watches movements of own hands before face and engages in finger play: beginning to clasp and unclasp hands, pressing palms of hands together.

Recognizes feeding bottle and makes eager welcoming movements as it approaches his face.

Regards small still objects within 6 to 10 inches for more than a second or two, but seldom fixates continuously.

Converges eyes as dangling ball is moved towards face.

Defensive blink clearly shown.

Holds rattle for few moments when placed in hand, may move towards face, sometimes bashing chin, but seldom (until 16 or 18 weeks) capable of regarding it at the same time.

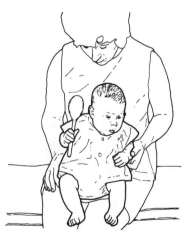

Follows moving ball in horizontal plane

Follows moving ball in vertical plane and converges eyes

Holds toy but cannot yet co-ordinate hand and eyes

Age 3 Months

Hearing and Speech

Sudden loud noises still distress, provoking blinking, screwing up of eyes, crying and turning away.

Definite quieting or smiling to sound of mother's voice before she touches him, but not when screaming.

Vocalizes delightedly when spoken to or pleased; also when alone.

Cries when uncomfortable or annoyed.

Quietens to sound of rattle of spoon in cup or if small bell rung gently out of sight for three to five seconds, with pauses of three to five seconds, at 6 to 12 inches on level with ear.

May turn eyes and/or head towards sound-source; brows may wrinkle and eyes dilate. May move head from side to side as if searching for sound-source.

Often sucks or licks lips in response to sounds of preparation for feeding.

Shows excitement at sound of approaching voices, footsteps, running bathwater, etc.

(*Note:* Deaf baby, instead, may obviously be startled by Mother's sudden appearance beside cot).

Social Behaviour and Play

Fixes eyes unblinkingly on mother's face when feeding, with contented purposeful gaze.

Beginning to react to familiar situations, showing by smiles, coos and excited movements that he recognizes preparations for feeds, baths, etc.

Now definitely enjoys bath and caring routines.

Responds with obvious pleasure to friendly handling, especially when accompanied by playful tickling and vocal sounds.

Mother supports at shoulders when dressing and bathing.

Turns towards meaningful sound

Turns to nearby voice

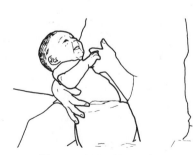

Happy response to mother

In supine raises head from pillow to look at feet.

Lifts legs into vertical and grasps one foot, or (later) two feet.

Sits with support in cot or pram and turns head from side to side to look around him.

Moves arms in brisk purposeful fashion and holds them up to be lifted.

When hands grasped, braces shoulders and pulls himself to sit.

Kicks strongly, legs alternating.

Can roll over front to back and (usually) back to front.

Held sitting, head is firmly erect and back straight.

May sit alone momentarily.

Placed in prone, lifts head and chest well up supporting himself on flattened palms and extended arms.

Held standing with feet touching hard surface, bears weight on feet and bounces up and down actively.

'Downward parachute' manoeuvre readily demonstrated.

Age 6 Months

Posture and
Large Movements

Supine, lifts legs and grasps foot

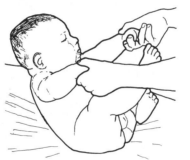
Pulled to sit, braces shoulders

Held sitting, back straight

Prone, arms extended

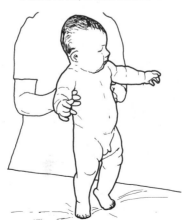
Held standing takes weight on legs

'Downward parachute' present

Age 6 Months

Vision and
Fine Movements

Visually insatiable: moves head and eyes eagerly in every direction when attention is attracted.

Follows adult's activities across room with purposeful alertness.

Eyes move in unison: any squint now definitely abnormal.

Immediately fixates interesting small objects within 6 to 12 inches, e.g. toy, bell, wooden cube, sweet, and almost simultaneously stretches out both hands to grasp them.

Uses whole hand to palmar grasp and passes toy from one hand to other.

When toys fall from hand within visual field, watches to resting place.

When toys fall outside visual fields, forgets them or searches only vaguely round cot with eyes and patting hands.

Watches rolling balls of 2- to quarter-inch (or less) diameter at 10 feet.

May also fixate mounted balls of similar sizes, but difficult to hold attention.

Brisk response to peripheral vision test from now on.

| *Grasps bell with both hands* | *Palmar grasp and transfer* | *Regards rolling ball at 5–10 feet* |

Turns immediately to mother's voice across room.

Vocalizes tunefully to self and others using sing-song vowel sounds or single and double 'syllables' e.g. a-a, muh, goo, der, adah, er-leh, aroo, etc.

Laughs, chuckles and squeals aloud in play.

Screams with annoyance.

Shows evidence of selective response to different emotional tones of mother's voice.

Responds to baby hearing tests at 1½ feet on ear level right and left by correct visual localization, but may show slightly brisker response on one side.

Tests employed—voice, rattle, cup and spoon, paper, bell: two seconds with two seconds' pause. Minimal intensity.

Hands competent to reach for and to grasp small toys.

Most often uses two-handed scooping-in approach, but occasionally a single hand.

Takes everything to mouth.

Finds feet as well as hands interesting to move about and regard: sometimes uses feet to help in grasping objects.

Puts hands to bottle and pats it when feeding.

Offered rattle, reaches for it immediately and shakes deliberately to make it sound, often regarding it closely at the same time.

Manipulates objects attentively passing them frequently from hand to hand.

Still friendly with strangers but occasionally shows some shyness or even slight anxiety when approached too nearly or abruptly, especially if mother is out of sight.

Definitely reserved with strangers from about seven months.

Age 6 Months

Hearing
and Speech

Social Behaviour
and Play

Delighted response to active play

Turns to minimal sound on ear level   *Turns to quiet voice*   *Still friendly with strangers*

Age 9 Months

Posture and
Large Movements

Sits alone for 10–15 minutes on floor.

Can lean forward to pick up a toy without losing balance.

Can turn body to look sideways while stretching out to grasp dangling toy or pick up toy from floor.

Very active movements of whole body and limbs in cot, pram and bath.

Progresses on floor by rolling or squirming.

Attempts to crawl: sometimes succeeds.

Pulls to stand holding on to support for a few moments, but cannot lower himself. Falls backwards with bump.

Held standing, steps purposefully on alternate feet.

'Forward parachute' manoeuvre present (from about seven months).

Sits on floor and manipulates toys

Attempts to crawl

Stands holding on

'Forward parachute' present

Visually very attentive to people, objects and happenings in his environment.

Immediately stretches out, one hand leading, to grasp a small toy, e.g. wooden block, when offered. Manipulates objects with lively interest, passing from hand to hand, turning over etc. Regards unoffered but accessible toy appraisingly before grasping, especially if unfamiliar.

Pokes at small sweet with index finger and beginning to point at more distant objects with same finger.

Grasps string between finger and thumb in scissor fashion to pull toy towards him.

Picks up small sweet between finger and thumb with 'inferior' pincer grasp.

Can release toy by dropping or by pressing against firm surface, but cannot yet place down voluntarily.

Looks in correct direction for falling and fallen toys, including those falling over edge of pram or table.

Watches activities of adults, children and animals within 10 to 12 feet with sustained interest for minutes at a time.

Watches rolling balls $\frac{1}{8}$ inches at 10 feet.

Fixates mounted balls down to $\frac{1}{8}$ inch at 10 feet but difficult to hold attention.

Age 9 Months

Vision and
Fine Movements

Pokes at pellet

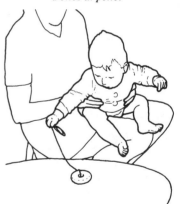

Grasps string scissor fashion

Lifts block but cannot place down   *Alert peripheral vision*   *Watches rolling balls at 10 feet*

Age 9 Months

Hearing and
Speech

Eagerly attentive to everyday sounds, particularly voice.

Vocalizes deliberately as a means of inter-personal communication in friendliness or annoyance.

Shouts to attract attention, listens, then shouts again.

Babbles loudly and tunefully in long repetitive strings of syllables (e.g. dad-dad, mam-mam, adaba, agaga.)

Babble is practised largely for self-amusement but also as a sign of favoured communication.

Understands 'no-no' and 'bye-bye'.

Imitates adults playful vocal and other sounds (e.g. smacking lips, cough, brr, and even word-like sounds of 'vowel and tune' type.)

Immediate localizing response to baby hearing tests at three feet from ear above and below ear level, but not in mid-line.

(*Note:* Deaf child's vocalizations remain at primitive level and do not usually progress to this repetitive tuneful babble. Meagre or monotonous vocalizations after eight or nine months should always arouse suspicion.)

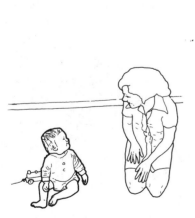

*Delighted imitation of playfull
vocalizations*

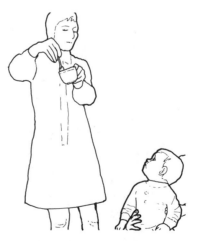

*Localizes lateral sounds below and
above ear level*

*Hears but cannot localize in
mid-line*

Holds, bites and chews a biscuit.

Puts hands round bottle or cup when feeding.

Tries to grasp spoon when being fed.

Throws body back and stiffens in annoyance or resistance, usually vocalizing protestingly at same time.

Clearly distinguishes strangers from familiars and requires reassurance before accepting their advances; clings to known adult and hides face.

Still takes everything to mouth.

Seizes bell in one hand; imitates ringing action, waving or banging it on table, (sometimes) pokes clapper, or 'drinks' from bowl.

Plays peek-a-bo and imitates hand-clapping.

Holds out toy grasped in hand to adult, but cannot yet give into adults' palm.

Finds toy which is partially hidden under cushion or cover while he watches.

May find toy wholly hidden under cup or cushion.

Mother supports only intermittently when dressing on her knee.

Sits safely upright on mother's arm when carried. Turns head to look around him.

Age 9 Months

Social Behaviour
and Play

Grasps bell by handle and rings in imitation

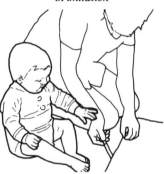

Watches while plaything is partly hidden

And promptly finds it

Watches while plaything is completely hidden

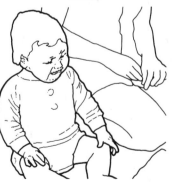

Cannot find it and is distressed

Age 12 Months

Posture and
Large Movements

Sits well on floor and for indefinite time.
Can rise to sitting position from lying down.
Crawls on hands and knees, shuffles on buttocks, or bear-walks rapidly about the floor.
Pulls to standing and lets himself down again holding onto furniture.
Walks round furniture lifting one foot and stepping sideways.
Walks forward and sideways with one or both hands held.
May stand alone for a few moments. May walk alone.
May crawl up stairs. (Averages 13 to 14 months.)

Vision and
Fine Movements

Picks up fine objects e.g. sweets, crumbs, string with neat pincer grasp between thumb and tip of index finger.
Drops and throws toys forward deliberately and watches them fall to ground.
Looks in correct place for toys which roll out of sight.
Points with index finger at objects he wishes to handle or happenings which interest him.
Watches small toy pulled along floor across room at 10 feet.
Out of doors watches movements of people, animals, motor cars, etc. with prolonged intent regard.
Recognizes familiars approaching from 20 feet or more.
Uses both hands freely but may show preferences for one.
Beginning to show interest in pictures.
Holds two cubes, one in each hand, simultaneously, with primitive 'tripod' grasp, and clicks together in imitation.
Watches rolling and mounted balls down to $\frac{1}{8}$ inch at 10 feet.

Walks one hand held

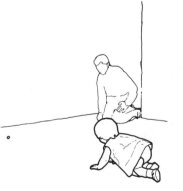

Crawls to retrieve rolling ball

Points to mounted ball in vision test

Knows and immediately turns to own name.

Jargons loudly and incessantly in 'conversational cadences'.

Vocalizations contain most vowels and many consonants.

Shows by suitable behaviour and response that he understands several words in usual context (e.g. own and family names, cup, spoon, ball, car, dinner, walk, pussy, etc.)

Comprehends simple instructions associated with gesture (e.g. 'give it to Daddy', 'come to Mummy', 'where are your shoes?', 'say bye-bye', 'clap hands', etc.)

Imitates adults' playful vocalizations and (sometimes) word forms with gleeful enthusiasm.

May hand adult common objects on request, e.g. spoon, cup, ball, shoe. Demonstrates 'definition by use'.

Immediate response to baby hearing tests at 3–4½ feet but rapidly habituates.

Age 12 Months

Hearing and
Speech

Full turn to voice

Definition-by-use of everyday objects

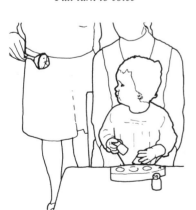

Turns to minimal sound of rattle

Quickly loses interest in same sound repeated

Turns eyes to same sound on other side

Age 12 Months

Social Behaviour
and Play

Explores every possibility of bell

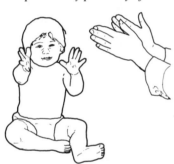

Plays pat-a-cake

Drinks from cup with little assistance. Chews.

Holds spoon but cannot yet use it by himself.

Helps with dressing by holding out arm for sleeve and foot for shoe.

Takes objects to mouth less often.

Ceasing to drool.

Puts wooden cubes in and out of cup or box when shown.

Rattles spoon in cup in imitation and often spontaneously.

Seizes bell by top of handle, rings briskly, manipulates rapidly and competently in every possible way.

Listens with obvious pleasure to sound-making toys and repeats appropriate activities to reproduce sounds.

Gives toys to adult on request and sometimes spontaneously.

Quickly finds toys hidden before his eyes.

Likes to be constantly within sight and hearing of familiar adult.

Demonstrates affection to familiars.

Plays 'pat-a-cake' and waves 'bye-bye' on request and the latter sometimes spontaneously.

Sits or sometimes stands without support while mother dresses.

Watches while toy is hidden under cup

Regards and reaches for cup

Promptly finds toy

Walks alone (usually) with uneven steps: feet wide apart, arms slightly flexed and held above head or at shoulder-level for balance.

Starts voluntarily but frequently stopped by falling or bumping into furniture.

Lets himself down from standing to sitting by collapsing backwards with a bump, or (sometimes) by falling forward on hands and then back to sitting. Can get to feet alone.

Creeps upstairs safely, and (sometimes) gets downstairs backwards, slowly.

Kneels unaided or with slight support on floor and in pram, cot and bath.

Picks up string, small sweets, crumbs etc. with precise pincer grasp, using either hand.

Manipulates cubes: builds tower of two cubes after demonstration.

Grasps crayon with (either) whole hand in palmar grasp and imitates to and fro scribble after demonstration.

Looks with interest at coloured pictures in book and pats page.

Follows with eyes path of small cube or small toy pulled across floor or swept vigorously from table to destination 10 to 12 feet away.

Demands desired objects out of his reach by imperious finger-pointing.

Stands at window and watches outside happening for several minutes, pointing to emphasize interest.

Watches rolling balls and fixates mounted balls down to $\frac{1}{8}$ inch.

Age 15 months

Posture and
Large Movements

Vision and
Fine Movements

Walks alone, feet apart, arms assisting balance

Manipulates blocks and builds tower of two

Shows definition-by-use of common objects

Age 15 months

Hearing and
Speech

Jabbers loudly and freely, using wide range of vocal tunes and phonetic units.

Speaks 2–6 or more recognizable words spontaneously in correct context and demonstrates understanding many more.

Communicates wishes and needs at table by pointing and vocalizing. Points to familiar persons, animals, toys etc. when requested. Definition-by-use of common objects.

Understands and obeys simple instructions (e.g. 'Don't touch', 'Come for dinner', 'Give me the ball', 'Kiss daddy goodnight').

Baby hearing tests at 4½–6 feet.

Social Behaviour
and Play

Holds and drinks from cup when adult holds and takes back.

Holds spoon, brings it to mouth and licks it, but (usually) cannot prevent it turning over. Chews well.

Helps more constructively with dressing.

Indicates when he has wet or soiled his pants.

Pushes large wheeled toy with handle on level ground.

Explores properties and possibilities of toys, convenient household objects and sound-makers with lively interest.

Seldom takes toys to mouth. Carries dolls by limbs, hair or clothing. Repeatedly casts objects to floor in play or rejection.

Physically restless and intensely curious regarding people, objects and events within his 'world' of sustained sensory attention.

Emotionally labile and closely dependent upon adult's reassuring presence.

Needs constant supervision for protection against dangers of extended exploration of environment, consequent upon his increased mobility.

Carries doll by leg

*Grasps crayon in palm and scribbles
to and fro lines*

Pushes large wheeled toy on level

Walks well with feet only slightly apart, starts and stops safely.

No longer needs to hold upper arms in extension to balance.

Runs carefully, head held erect in midline, eyes fixed on ground one to two yards ahead, but (usually) cannot continue round obstacles.

Pushes and pulls large toys, boxes etc. round floor.

Chooses to carry large doll or teddy-bear (sometimes two) while walking.

Backs into small chair or slides in sideways to seat himself.

Climbs forward into adults' chair then turns round and sits.

Walks upstairs with helping hand (often downstairs).

Creeps backwards downstairs or (occasionally) bumps down a few steps on buttocks facing forwards.

Kneels upright on flat surface without support.

Flexes knees and hips in squatting position to pick up toy from floor and (usually) with hands helping, rises to feet alone.

Age 18 Months

Posture and
Large Movements

Walks well carrying toy

Pushes and pulls wheeled toy

Climbs into adult chair

Walks up and down stairs with help

Squats to pick up fallen toy

Age 18 Months

Vision and
Fine Movements

Picks up small sweets, beads, pins, threads, etc. immediately on sight, with delicate pincer grasp.

Holds pencil in mid-shaft or at proximal end in palmar or primitive tripod grasp.

Spontaneous to and fro scribble and dots, using preferred or other hand alone or (sometimes) with pencils in both hands.

Builds tower of three cubes after demonstration (sometimes spontaneously).

Enjoys simple picture books, often recognizing and putting finger on boldly-coloured items on page.

Turns pages, several at a time.

Fixes eyes on small dangling toy at 10 feet and watches circular or pendulum movement briefly.

May tolerate this test with each eye separately.

Points to distant interesting objects out of doors.

Beginning to show preference for using one hand.

Watches and retrieves rolling balls to $\frac{1}{8}$ inch at 10 feet.

Fixates mounted balls at 10 feet to $\frac{1}{8}$ inch but attention easily distracted.

Possibly recognizes and names special Stycar miniature toys at 10 feet.

Retrieves rolling balls at 10 feet   *Builds tower of 3 bricks*   *Enjoys picture books*

Jabbers loudly and continually to himself at play employing wide range of pitch, with 'conversational' tunes and emotional inflections.

Attends to spoken communications addressed directly to him.

Uses 6–20+ recognizable words and understands many more.

Echoes prominent or last word in short sentences addressed to him.

Demands a desired object by pointing accompanied by loud, urgent vocalizations or single words.

Enjoys nursery rhymes and tries to join in.

Attempts to sing.

Hands named familiar objects correctly.

Obeys simple instructions e.g. 'get daddy's shoes', 'shut the door', 'where's pussy-cat'.

Shows his own or doll's hair, shoes, nose, feet.

Possibly special five-toy test. Possibly four animals Stycar picture test. Doll vocabulary and common objects language tests.

Age 18 Months

Hearing and
Speech

Vocabulary rapidly increasing   *Responds to free-field audiometer*   *Points to daddy's nose*

Age 18 Months

Social Behaviour
and Play

Holds spoon and gets food safely to mouth. Chews well.

Holds cup between both hands. Drinks without much spilling.

Lifts cup alone but (usually) hands back to adult when finished.

Takes off shoes, socks, hat. Seldom able to replace.

Still wets pants but beginning to give notice of urgent toilet needs by restlessness and vocalization.

Bowel control often attained (very variable).

Explores environment energetically and with increasing understanding.

No longer takes toys to mouth.

Remembers where objects belong.

Still casts objects to floor in play or anger but less often and seldom troubling visually to verify arrival on target.

Briefly imitates simple, everyday activities, e.g. feeding doll, reading book, brushing floor, washing clothes.

Plays contentedly alone but likes to be near familiar adult or older sibling.

Enjoys putting small objects in and out of containers.

Emotionally still very dependent upon familiar adult, especially mother.

Alternates between clinging and resistance.

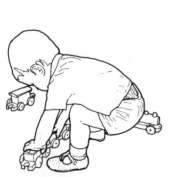

Plays alone contentedly with floor toys

Explores environment energetically

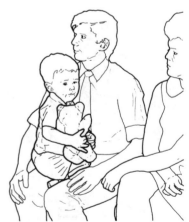

Still very dependent upon familiar adults

Runs safely on whole foot, stopping and starting with ease and avoiding obstacles.

Squats with complete steadiness to rest or to play with object on ground and rises to feet without using hands.

Pushes and pulls large, wheeled toys easily forwards and (usually) able to walk backwards pulling handle.

Pulls small wheeled toy by cord with obvious appreciation of direction.

Climbs on furniture to look out of window, or to open doors etc. and can get down again.

Shows increasing understanding of size of self in relation to size and position of objects in his environment and to enclosed spaces e.g. cupboards, barrels etc.

Walks upstairs and (often) down, holding onto rail or wall; two feet to a step.

Throws small ball overhand forwards without falling.

Walks into large ball when trying to kick it.

Sits on small tricycle, but cannot use pedals. Propels vehicle forwards with feet on floor.

Age 2 Years

Posture and
Large Movements

Gets up and down stairs

Walks into large ball

Sits and steers but cannot yet use pedals

Age 2 Years

Vision and
Fine Movements

Picks up pins, thread etc. accurately and quickly and places down neatly with increasing skill.

Removes paper wrapping from small sweet efficiently.

Builds tower of six or seven cubes.

Holds a pencil (usually) in preferred hand, well down shaft towards point using thumb and first two fingers.

Spontaneous circular scribble as well as to and fro scribble and dots.

Imitates vertical line and (sometimes) V shape.

Enjoys picture books, recognizing fine details in favourite pictures.

Turns pages singly.

Recognizes familiar adults in photograph after once shown but not (usually) self as yet.

Hand preference usually obvious.

Immediately catches sight of and names special miniature Stycar toys at 10 feet.

Will now usually tolerate this test with each eye separately.

Watches and retrieves rolling balls to ⅛ inch at 10 feet.

Fixates mounted balls to ⅛ inch at 10 feet.

Occasionally performs Stycar five-letter matching test.

Builds tower of 6 or 7 bricks

Holds pencil and scribbles

Enjoys books and turns pages singly

Matches miniature toys in vision test

Uses 50 or more recognizable words and obviously understands many more.

Attends to communications addressed to himself. Beginning to listen with obvious interest to more general talk.

Puts two or more words together to form simple sentences.

Refers to self by name.

Talks to self continually in long monologues as he plays but much is still incomprehensible to others.

Echolalia almost constant with one or more stressed words repeated.

Constantly asking names of objects and people.

Joins in nursery rhymes and songs.

Shows correctly and repeats words for hair, hand, feet, nose, eyes, mouth, shoes on request.

Hands and names familiar objects and pictures on request.

Carries out simple instructions 'tell daddy tea is ready', 'see what the postman has brought'.

Beginning to show meaningful assembly and definition-by-use of dolls-house sized toys.

Stycar six-toy test, four animals picture test. House or car picture test.

Play audiometry in free field possible.

Age 2 Years

Hearing and
Speech

Identifies named toys in hearing test　　*Play audiometry in free-field possible; listening*　　*Responds appropriately to free-field audiometry*

Age 2 Years

Social Behaviour
and Play

Spoon-feeds without spilling. Chews competently.

Lifts cup, drinks and replaces it on table without difficulty.

Asks for food and drink.

Puts on hat and shoes.

Verbalizes toilet needs in reasonable time.

Usually dry through day (variable).

Intensely curious regarding environment. Turns door handles and often runs outside. Little comprehension of common dangers.

Follows mother round house and imitates domestic activities in simultaneous play.

Spontaneously engages in simple role or situational make-believe activities.

Constantly demanding mother's attention.

Clings tightly in affection, fatigue or fear.

Resistive and rebellious when thwarted.

Tantrums when frustrated or in trying to make himself understood but attention (usually) readily distracted.

Defends own possessions with determination.

Has as yet, no idea of sharing playthings or adults' attention.

Plays quite contentedly near other children but not with them.

Resentful of attention shown to other children particularly by his own familiars.

No understanding of need to defer or modify immediate satisfaction of wishes.

Lifts and replaces cup safely

Puts on hat (and shoes)

Engages in simple 'pretend' play

Plays near others but not with them

All locomotor skills rapidly improving.

Walks upstairs confidently and (usually) downstairs holding rail, two feet to step.

Runs well straight forward and climbs easy nursery apparatus.

Pushes and pulls large toys skilfully but may have difficulty in steering them round obstacles.

Can jump with two feet together from low step: can stand on tiptoe if shown.

Casts hand ball somewhat stiffly at body level. Kicks large ball, but gently and lopsidedly.

Picks up pins, threads etc., with each eye covered separately.

Builds tower of seven-plus cubes using preferred and helping hand.

Recognizes minute details in picture books.

Holds pencil in preferred hand, with improved tripod grasp.

Imitates horizontal line and circle, also (usually) T and V.

Recognizes miniature toys at 10 feet with each eye separately.

Recognizes self in photographs when once shown.

May also match first block of special Stycar single letter cards, i.e. V O T H X, to smallest size at 10 feet.

Age 2½ years

Posture and
Large Movements

Vision and
Fine Movements

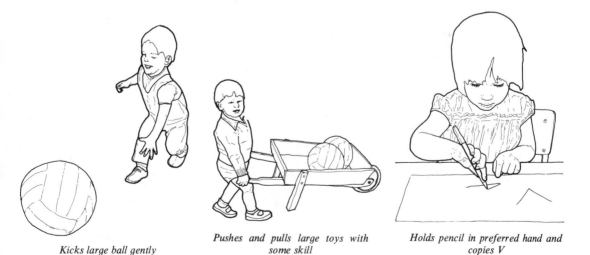

Kicks large ball gently

Pushes and pulls large toys with some skill

Holds pencil in preferred hand and copies V

Age 2½ years

**Hearing and
Speech**

Uses 200 or more recognizable words, but speech shows numerous infantilisms of articulation and sentence structure.

Knows full name. Talks audibly and intelligibly to self at play, concerning events happening here and now. Echolalia persists.

Continually asking questions beginning 'What?' 'Who?'. Uses pronouns I, Me and You correctly.

Stuttering in eagerness common. Says a few nursery rhymes. Enjoys simple familiar stories read from picture book.

Plays meaningfully with miniature (doll's-house size) toys adding intelligent running commentary.

Stycar Hearing and Language Tests: Four animals picture tests, 1st cube test, 6-toy test, full doll vocabulary, house and car picture test.

**Social Behaviour
and Play**

Eats skilfully with spoon and may use fork.

Pulls down pants or knickers at toilet, but seldom able to replace.

Usually dry through night, if lifted (very variable).

Exceedingly active, restless and resistive of restraint. Has little understanding of common dangers or need to defer immediate wishes.

Throws tantrums when thwarted and less easily distracted. Emotionally still very dependent on adult.

More sustained role play (putting dolls to bed, washing clothes, driving motor cars etc.) but with frequent reference to a friendly adult. Watches other children at play interestedly, occasionally joins in for a few minutes, but as yet has little notion of necessity to share playthings or adults' attention.

Enjoys picture books and stories

*Active and curious with little notion
of common dangers*

Simple make-believe play

Walks alone upstairs with alternating feet and downstairs, two feet to a step.

Usually jumps from bottom step (two feet together).

Climbs nursery apparatus with agility.

Can turn round obstacles and corners while running and also while pushing and pulling large toys.

Walks forwards, backwards, sideways, etc., hauling large toys with complete confidence.

Obviously appreciates size and movements of own body in relation to external objects and space.

Rides tricycle, using pedals, and can steer it round wide corners.

Can stand and walk on tiptoe.

Stands momentarily on one (preferred) foot when shown.

Sits with feet crossed at ankles.

Can throw ball overhand and catch large ball on or between extended arms. Kicks ball forcibly.

Age 3 Years

Posture and
Large Movements

Walks upstairs and down carrying large toy　　　*Jumps from bottom step (2 feet)*　　　*Stands on one foot momentarily*

Age 3 Years

Vision and
Fine Movements

Picks up pins, threads etc. willingly with each eye covered separately.

Builds tower of nine cubes and (by $3\frac{1}{2}$ years) one or more bridges of three from model using two hands co-operatively.

Threads large wooden beads on shoe lace.

Can close fist and wiggle thumb in imitation, right and left.

Holds pencil in preferred hand near point between first two fingers and thumb and uses with good control.

Copies circle (also V H T). Imitates cross.

Draws man with head and usually indication of one or two other features or parts.

Matches two or three primary colours (usually red and yellow correct, but may confuse blue and green).

May know names of colours.

Enjoys painting with large brush on easel, covering whole paper with wash of colour or painting primitive 'pictures' which are (usually) named during or after production.

Cuts with scissors.

Recognizes special miniature Stycar toys at 10 feet. Performs Stycar single letter vision test at 10 feet, five or seven letters and near card to bottom.

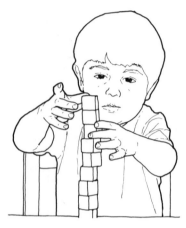

Builds tower of 9 or 10 bricks

Builds several bridges from model

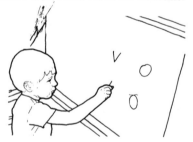

Copies circle and V

Cuts with scissors

Matches letters on key card

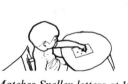

Matches Snellen letters at 10 feet (5 or 7)

Speech modulating in loudness and range of pitch.

Large vocabulary intelligible even to strangers, but speech still shows many infantile phonetic substitutions and unconventional grammatical forms.

Gives full name and sex and (sometimes) age.

Uses personal pronouns and plurals correctly and most prepositions.

Still talks to self in long monologues mostly concerned with immediate present, including make-believe activities.

Carries on simple conversations and able briefly to describe present activities and past experiences.

Asks many questions beginning 'what', 'where', and 'who'.

Listens eagerly to stories and demands favourites over and over again.

Knows several nursery rhymes to repeat and (sometimes) sing.

Counts by rote up to 10 or more, but little appreciation of quantity beyond two or three.

Stycar tests. Hearing: seven-toy test, four animals pictures, first or second cube test, six 'high-frequency' word pictures.

Language: everyday things, auditory discrimination pictures, scattered balls test.

*Co-operates in hearing and speech
tests with pictures*

*Co-operates in conventional
pure-tone audiometric test*

Age 3 Years

Social Behaviour
and Play

Eats with fork and spoon.

Washes hands but needs supervision in drying.

Can pull pants and knickers down and up but needs help with buttons and other fastenings.

Dry through night (very variable).

General behaviour more amenable. Affectionate and confiding.

Likes to help adult in domestic activities, gardening, shopping etc.

Makes effort to keep surroundings tidy.

Vividly realized make-believe play, including invented people and objects.

Enjoys floor-play with bricks, boxes, toy trains, dolls, prams, etc. alone or with siblings.

Joins in active make-believe play with other children.

Understands sharing playthings, sweets, etc.

Shows affection for younger siblings.

Shows some appreciation of difference between present and past and of need to defer satisfaction of wishes to future.

Washes and dries hands under supervision

Can pull pants down and up

Vivid make-believe social play

Walks (or runs) alone up and down stairs, one foot to step.

Navigates self-locomotion skilfully, turning sharp corners, running pushing and pulling.

Climbs ladders and trees.

Can stand, walk and run on tiptoe.

Expert rider of tricycle, executing sharp U turns easily.

Stands on one (preferred) foot three or five seconds and hops on preferred foot.

Arranges and picks up objects from floor by bending from waist with knees extended.

Sits with knees crossed.

Shows increasing skill in ball games throwing, catching, bouncing, kicking, etc. including use of bat.

Age 4 Years

Posture and
Large Movements

Up and down stairs in adult
fashion

Climbs trees

Stands and runs on tiptoe

Hops on one foot

Age 4 Years

Vision and
Fine Movements

Picks up and replaces very small items, e.g. pins, thread, crumbs etc. with each eye covered separately.

Threads small beads to make necklaces, if adult threads needle.

Builds tower of 10 or more cubes and several bridges of three from one model on request or spontaneously.

Builds three steps with six cubes after demonstration.

Imitates spreading of hand and bringing thumb into opposition with each finger in turn right and left.

Holds and uses pencil with good control in adult fashion. Copies cross (also V H T O).

Draws a man with head, legs and trunk, and (usually) arms and fingers.

Draws recognizable house on request or spontaneously. Beginning to name drawings before production.

Matches and names four primary colours correctly.

Stycar single letter vision test at 10 feet. Seven letters. Also near test card to bottom.

Builds several bridges from memory

Builds 3 steps after demonstration

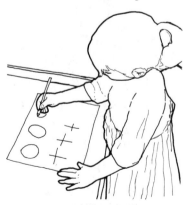

Copies circles and crosses

Vision easily tested (here in mirror)

Speech grammatically correct and completely intelligible.

Shows only a few infantile phonetic substitutions usually of r-l-w-y group or p-th-f-s group or k-t sound group.

Gives connected account of recent events and experiences.

Gives full name, home address and (usually) age.

Eternally asking questions 'why?', 'when?', 'how?' and meanings of words.

Listens to and tells long stories, sometimes confusing fact and fantasy.

Counts by rote up to 20 or more, and beginning to count objects by word and touch in (one to one) correspondence up to four or five.

Enjoys jokes and verbal incongruities.

Knows several nursery rhymes which he repeats or sings correctly.

Stycar hearing tests: seven toys, picture vocabulary tests: six or 12 pictures.

Language tests: full range, including story.

Age 4 Years

Hearing and
Speech

Enjoys looking at books and hearing stories

Co-operates in pure-tone audiometry

Age 4 Years

Social Behaviour
and Play

Eats skilfully with spoon and fork.

Washes and dries hands. Brushes teeth.

Can undress and dress except for laces, ties and back buttons.

General behaviour more independent and strongly self-willed.

Inclined to verbal impertinence with adults and quarrelling with playmates when wishes crossed.

Shows sense of humour in talk and activities.

Dramatic make-believe play and dressing-up favoured.

Floor games very complicated but habits less tidy.

Constructive out-of-door building with any materials available.

Needs companionship of other children with whom he is alternately co-operative and aggressive as with adults, but understands need to argue with words rather than blows.

Understands taking turns as well as sharing.

Shows concern for younger siblings and sympathy for playmates in distress.

Appreciates past, present and future time.

*Washes and dries hands
competently*

Dresses and undresses alone

*Understands need for taking turns
in play*

Walks easily on narrow line.

Runs lightly on toes.

Active and skilful in climbing, sliding, swinging, digging and various 'stunts'.

Skips on alternate feet.

Moves rhythmically to music.

Can stand on one foot eight to 10 seconds right and left and (usually) also stand on preferred foot, with arms folded.

Can hop two or three yards forwards on each foot separately.

Grips strongly with either hand.

Can bend and touch toes without flexing knees.

Plays all varieties of ball games with considerable ability, including those requiring appropriate placement or scoring, according to accepted rules.

Age 5 Years

Posture and
Large Movements

Walks on narrow line

Stands on one foot with arms folded

Age 5 Years

Vision and
Fine Movements

Builds 3 or 4 steps from model

Copies square and cross

Picks up and replaces minute objects when each eye is covered separately.

Builds three steps with six cubes from model (sometimes four steps from 10 cubes).

Threads large needles alone and sews real stitches.

Good control in writing and drawing of pencils and paint brushes.

Copies square and (at 5½ years) triangle. (Also letters **V T H O X L A C U Y**.)

Writes a few letters spontaneously.

Draws recognizable man with head, trunk, legs, arms and features.

Draws house with door, windows, roof and chimney.

Spontaneously produces many other pictures containing several items and usually indication of background of environment. Names before production.

Colours pictures neatly, staying within outlines.

Counts fingers on one hand with index finger of other.

Names four primary colours or more and matches 10 or 12 colours.

Stycar vision tests: full nine-letter vision chart at 20 feet and near-vision testing card to bottom, letters named copied or matched). Peripheral vision test.

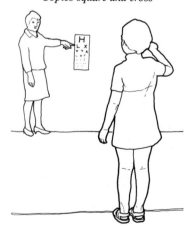

Distant vision test at 20 feet

Near vision test

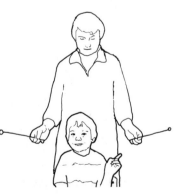

Peripheral vision test

Speech fluent, grammatically conventional and (usually) phonetically correct except for confusions of s, f, th group.

Delights in reciting or singing rhymes and jingles.

Loves to be read or told stories and acts them out in detail later, alone or with friends.

Gives full name, age and (usually) birthday. Gives home address.

Defines concrete nouns by use.

Constantly asks meaning of abstract words and uses them in and out of season.

Enjoys jokes and riddles.

Stycar hearing tests: twelve 'high-frequency' picture vocabulary or word lists. Third cube test, six sentences.

Language tests: full range.

Age 5 Years

Hearing and
Speech

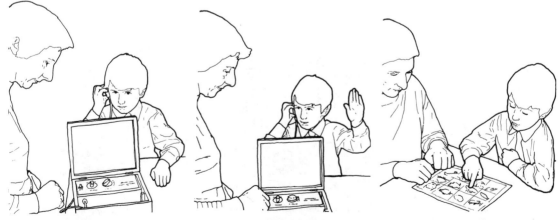

Pure tone audiometry—listening   *Pure tone audiometry—hearing*   *Hearing and speech picture test*

Age 5 Years

Social Behaviour
and Play

Uses knife and fork competently.

Washes and dries face and hands but needs help or supervision for the rest.

Undresses and dresses alone.

General behaviour more sensible, controlled and independent.

Comprehends need for order and tidiness, but needs constant reminder.

Domestic and dramatic play continued alone or with playmates from day to day.

Floor games very complicated.

Plans and builds constructively in and out of doors.

Chooses own friends.

Co-operative with companions most of the time and understands need for rules and fair play.

Shows definite sense of humour.

Appreciates meaning of clock-time in relation to daily programme.

Tender and protective towards younger children and pets.

Comforts playmates in distress.

Engages in elaborate make-believe group play

Affectionate and helpful to younger siblings

Development of Visual Competence

This is the reception of mobile and static patterns of light, shade and hue by the eye, and their transmission to the occipital region of the central nervous system. It depends upon structural and functional adequacy of the eye and its connections.

Seeing

This is paying attention to what is seen with the object of interpreting its meaning. It depends upon capacity and opportunity to benefit from experience. Visual function can be voluntarily suspended by closing the eyes.

Looking

Has not seen before birth but rapidly adapts.
    Pupils react to light.
    Lids close against intense light.
    'Doll's eye' reflex present.
    Eyes and head turn to diffuse light.
    Limited powers of accommodation produce relatively fixed focal length of 8 to 12 inches until four to six weeks.
    Follows dangling ball briefly at focal distance.
    Consistent watching of mother's face when feeding from about three weeks.
    Eyes often 'corner' reflexly in direction of sound-source, therefore TEST VISION FIRST, with silent object.

Neonate

Regards nearby human face with intense pre-occupation.
    Scans surroundings when held upright and no face in view.
    Follows slowly moving dangling ball at 6–10 inches from face attentively.
    Defensive blink present from about 4–6 weeks.
    Converges eyes for finger-play from 3 months.

1–3 Months

Visually very alert for near and far.
    Smooth following eye movements for dangling ball in all directions.
    Regards small pellet on table-top and approaches with hand.
    Reaches for toys (from $4\frac{1}{2}$ months) grasps firmly and regards closely.

4–6 Months

Peripheral vision easily tested.
Watches objects moving or falling within visual fields.
Both eyes working as a team.
Squint now definitely abnormal however slight and transient.

7–12 Months

Visual competence for near and far rapidly improving.
Picks up pellets between finger and thumb with increasing skill.
Follows dangling ball in all directions.
Anticipates rotating ball (from 9 to 10 months).
Looks for fallen toys and toys hidden while watching (from 9 to 10 months).
Tests with rolling balls (usually) and mounted balls (probably) applicable down to $\frac{3}{16}$ or $\frac{1}{8}$ inch at 10 feet.
Brisk response to peripheral vision test.

1–2 Years

Probably has full adult visual acuity for rolling and mounted balls but difficult to hold attention for prolonged tests owing to increasing visual sophistication and need for meaningful reinforcements. Picks up threads and small pellets.

2–3½ Years

Matching tests with miniature toys (2 years onwards) and Stycar single letter test five letters (2½ years onwards) applicable at 10 feet. Also near test card to end.

3½–4½ Years

Stycar single letter test—seven letters (matching) at 10 feet. Also near test card to end.

4–7 Years

Stycar nine letters (single letters or charts) *under* five years at 10 feet *over* five years at 20 feet. Also near test card to end.

Performance at school entry: *Superior:* naming i.e. reading letters
(4½–5½ years)

Average: drawing in the air i.e. copying

Immature: (at 5 years) matching.

Recommendations

Begin with ambi-ocular testing (i.e. both eyes uncovered) to ensure co-operation.
Test each eye separately at first visit, if possible.
Near vision tests always desirable, particularly when other members of the family have visual defects.

Peripheral vision should always be checked.

Colour vision tests desirable for boys.

Remember possibility of visuo-spatial and visuo-motor defects in multi-handicapped children and in those showing difficulty in block building, bead threading, brushwork, reading, writing or spelling or in copy-design or draw-a-man tests.

Development of Hearing and Listening

Hearing

This is the reception of sound by the ear and its transmission to the central nervous system. It is present before birth and, therefore, the first of the distant receptors to function.

Listening

This is paying attention to what is heard with the object of interpreting its meaning.

Birth to 3 Months

'Startle' and 'freezing' reflexes present from birth.
Eyes often 'corner' reflexly in direction of sound source.
Therefore, ALWAYS TEST VISION FIRST.
Turns head to regard nearby speaker about 4–6 weeks.
By 8–10 weeks attends to meaningful sounds (e.g. spoon-in-cup) and reacts appropriately.
Cries (birth), coos (4–6 weeks) and chuckles (10–12 weeks).

4–7 Months

Consistent auditory localizing response to quiet voice and sound-making objects at 1½ feet on ear level.
Own vocalizations frequent, loud and tuneful showing single and double 'syllables'.
Shouts to attract attention (5–6 months).

8–12 Months

Increasing competent localization for sound-making devices above and below ear level at 3–6 feet.
Babbles in long repetitive 'strings' of syllables (dad-dad, ababa, mam-mam etc.). (7–8 months onwards).
Imitates adults playful sounds including occasional word forms (9–10 months).
Knows and turns to own name. May recognize a few other names.
Responds suitably to everyday familiar sounds.

12–18 Months

Alert to very quiet meaningful sounds but soon becomes bored when sounds repeated without interesting result.
Turns to voice appropriately. Obeys very simple instructions.
May also react to pure-tones in free field.
Jargons continually at play, using cadences of speech.

Begins to use a few recognizable words in correct context about 14–15 months.

Tests with interest-holding sound-making devices remain useful.	18 Months–2½ Years

Child's own spontaneous listening behaviour and vocal utterances provide best indicators of auditory competence.

Understands simple spoken information and instructions.

Begins putting words together in short sentences from about 20–22 months.

Conventional hearing and speech tests employing picture vocabularies play audiometry etc. increasingly applicable.	2½–4½ Years

Grammar usually correct by 4½ years.

Comprehension of spoken language and span of auditory attention should be tested.

Child's own speech and sentence construction should be heard and evaluated.

In babies and handicapped children, always test vision before hearing.	Recommendations

Always record separately what is observed personally and what is reported by others with regard to reactions to sound and use of speech.

Review techniques and instruments employed at regular intervals.

_____

(See notes in the following section and on page 70.)

Stycar Hearing and Language Tests.
Materials and manuals of instruction are published by NFER (copyright).

Development of Communication

Terminology

It is essential to distinguish between hearing and listening; between prelinguistic (non-codemic) and linguistic (co-demic) communication; and between speech and spoken language.

Language codes may be received and expressed in words, mime, drawings or models.

Birth to 3 Months

Crying brings relief from distress.

First social communication in eye-to-eye contact (2–3 weeks onwards).

Social smile (4–6 weeks) with responsive vocalizations (6 weeks onwards, increasingly).

3–6 Months

Responds happily to all friendly comers (up to 6 months).

Loud, tuneful vocalizations to self and others when pleased, employing one or two syllables and wide range of pitch (4 months onwards).

Noisy protesting cries when distressed or annoyed.

Chuckles and laughs (3 months). Shouts to attract attention (5 months).

6–12 Months

Shows increasing reserve with strangers but very responsive to familiars.

Deliberately employs cadenced vocalizations as means of interpersonal communications.

Babbles in long repetitive strings of syllables for self-amusement when alone (7 months onwards) as well as to other people. This is a *very significant sign*.

Adults' actions with appropriate vocal accompaniments imitated and repeated for applause (9 months onwards).

Responds to own name and possibly recognizes a few others (10 months).

Demonstrates affection to familiars (11–12 months).

Calls attention to needs and interesting events by pointing and vocalizing (10 months onwards).

Spontaneous 'definition by use' of common objects applied to self (11–12 months).

Understands simple instructions employing combined words and gestures.

Continuous, loud, tuneful 'conversation-like' jargon to self and others (12 months onwards).

Imitates vocal tones just heard, including occasional word sounds.

Spontaneous use of single words in correct context (about 14 months).

Very dependent upon familiar adults.

1–1½ Years

Understands most of the simple language addressed to him.

Puts 2 or 3 words together to form meaningful sentences (about 21 months).

Talks continually to self and others while playing, but much is unintelligible even to familiars.

Echoes stressed or final words in speech of others.

Refers to self and others by name but beginning to use personal pronouns.

Beginning to ask questions (what? where?) and offer simple information (about 24 months).

Brief role or situational 'make-believe' play alone or with co-operative elder.

1½–2½ Years

Speech increasingly intelligible even to strangers, but still shows numerous infantilisms.

Vocabulary rapidly extending. Understands many more words than he uses.

Constantly asking questions (who? why?).

Self-talk during play decreasing in favour of talk addressed to others (3 years onwards).

'Stammering of eagerness' common, but transient.

Uses pronouns and easier prepositions correctly.

Engages in make-believe play with siblings or familiar playmates.

2½–4 Years

Speech fully intelligible; shows only minor infantile mis-pronounciations.

Possesses extensive vocabulary. Narrates long stories.

Correct grammatical usage established (about 4½ years).

Constantly asking questions (how? when?) and meanings of words.

Needs playmates of own age to invent, share, take turns, argue and reason with.

4 Years

Recommendations

Good history taking is the first essential.

Remember that children *learn* to speak by ear from adults and in meaningful situations. They *practice* on their age peers.

Always check child has adequate opportunity to hear and be heard.

In the record, distinguish carefully between what is personally heard and observed of the child's vocal utterances and other communications and what is reported by others.

Warning Signals,
re Hearing and Speaking

Prompt investigations are needed for:

1. All children known to be at risk of deafness.

2. Any suspicion on mother's part that child is not hearing normally.

3. NOT responding to nearby voices or everyday sounds by 6–8 weeks.

4. NOT showing ordinary interest in people and for playthings by 3–4 months.

5. NOT using frequent, tuneful, repetitive babble to self and others by 10 months (average 7–8 months).

6. NOT speaking single words by 21 months (average 13–15 months).

7. NOT putting 2 or 3 words together in sentences by 27 months (average 18–22 months).

8. NOT using intelligible speech by 4 years (average $3-3\frac{1}{2}$ years).

9. NOT demonstrating conventional grammatical usage by 5 years (average $4-4\frac{1}{2}$ years).

10. Still demonstrating articulation defects at $6\frac{1}{2}$ years.

Motor development

Postures and movements of limbs and trunk dominated by primary reflexes.	0–6 Weeks

Prone: turns head to one side, buttocks high with hips flexed, knees under abdomen, arms close to body, elbows flexed, hands fisted.

Supine: tonic neck reflex posture with head to one side, limbs on face side extended, on skull side flexed.

Pulled to sit: marked head lag present. Spine in one curve.

Placing reflexes and primary walking present.

Gradual disappearance of primary reflexes is accompanied by increasing control of neck and shoulder muscles.	6 Weeks to 3 Months

Prone: raises chin above table-top with increasing strength. Buttocks gradually lowered to flat while hips and knees extend. Elbows flexed away from body. Rests on forearms.

Supine: head in midline, limbs move symmetrically.

Hands open, brought together in finger play (3 months).

Pulled to sit: no head lag, lumbar curve (3 months).

Held standing: sags at knees (2–3 months).

Prone: gradually lifts head and chest higher above table top until (6 months) supports on flat palms and extended arms.	3–6 Months

Supine: lifts head from pillow (4½ months), moves limbs vigorously. Reaches out for toys (4½ months). Lifts legs to vertical (5 months). Grasps feet (5½–6 months).

Stretches out arms to be lifted (5½ months).

Pulled to sit: braces shoulders and assists. Head well controlled. Back straight. Sits with support (5½ months).

Held standing: takes weight on extended legs.

Bounces vigorously (6 months).

'Downward parachute' obtainable (5 months).

Prone: attempts to crawl (7–8 months). Rolls over front to back (6 months) and back to front (6½ months).	6–9 Months

Supine: dislikes position unless sleepy or actively playing with cot toys, using hands and feet to reach for and hold them.

Sitting: pulls self to sit in pram (from 7 months).

Sits on floor with support of own arms (7 months), without support (8 months).

Reaches for toys in front, upwards and to side without falling over (9 months).

Pulls to stand holding on to furniture (9 months), but cannot let self down so falls with bump.

Attempts to crawl (8 months onwards).

'Forward parachute' obtainable (7 months).

9–12 Months

Sits on floor for long periods, reaches for toys in front, to side, upwards and pivots to reach toy behind back. Rises to sit from supine (12 months).

Crawls rapidly (10–11 months), may crawl upstairs (12 months).

Pulls to stand, 'cruises', stepping sideways, and lets self down safely, holding on to furniture (11–12 months).

Walks with hand(s) held (11–12 months).

12–15 Months

Walks alone (13–14 months) broad base, uneven steps, arms held up to balance. Tumbles frequently.

Rapidly gains skill with practice.

Kneels on floor alone or with slight support.

Crawls upstairs (13 months) but (usually) not yet downstairs.

15–18 Months

Walks well and often runs. (18 months) stops and starts safely.

Pulls and pushes large wheeled toys (16 months).

Crawls upstairs and (backwards) downstairs. Walks upstairs with helping hand (18 months).

Picks up toy from floor without falling and rises to feet alone.

Backs or slides sideways into small chair to seat himself.

Climbs forward into adult chair and turns round.

2 Years

Runs well, stops and starts safely.

Walks upstairs with hand on wall two feet to step (2 years).

Usually crawls downstairs until 3 or 4 months later.

Squats to play with toys on floor.

Climbs on furniture.

2½ Years

Walks up and downstairs with hand on wall, two feet to step.

Climbs easy nursery apparatus.

Sits on pedal cycle and steers, but still propels with feet on floor.

Walks upstairs with alternating feet, downstairs 2 feet to step with(out) support.
    Can walk on tiptoe.
    Stands momentarily on one foot.
    Climbs nursery apparatus capably.
    Rides pedal cycle and turns wide corners.

3 Years

Walks easily up and downstairs with alternating feet.
    Runs on tiptoe.
    Climbs ladders, trees and high playground equipment.
    Rides pedal cycle quickly and turns sharp corners.
    Stands on one foot 3–5 seconds.

4 Years

Walks along chalked line.
    Runs up and down stairs.
    Climbs trees etc. skilfully and performs numerous 'stunts'.
    Stands on one foot 8–10 seconds (R and L) and (usually) with folded arms 3–4 seconds.
    Hops and skips on one foot (R and L).

5 Years

For detailed development of manipulative skills which evolve more variably, see full text.

Paediatric Developmental Examinations

Preliminary Screening (PDPS)	Suitable for *general use* at specified key ages. Must be simple in application, clear-cut in response, easy to record and reliable in result.
Diagnostic Evaluation (PDDA)	Suitable for regular use in *Development Clinics* (based in hospitals or community) by appropriately-trained and experienced medical practitioners. Necessitates availability of usual district hospital facilities and full community services.
Comprehensive Assessment (PDCA)	Suitable for use in specially designed *Regional Centres* by multi-professional team under the leadership of a senior consultant paediatrician. Necessitates availability of full teaching-hospital facilities and maintenance of close relations with hospital units and community services in catchment areas.

Outline of Paediatric Developmental Evaluation

Paediatric Examination	History, Measurements. Conventional medical examination.
Developmental Testing Procedures	Postures and large movements (head, trunk, four limbs). Manipulations (R and L hands). Vision (R and L, near and far) eye movements, peripheral vision (colour vision). Hearing (R and L, close and distant). Vocalizations and language of communication. Social competence: Self-care (feeding, dressing, toilet); Self-occupation (spontaneous and guided); Personal relationships (familiars and strangers).
Overall Deductions	General understanding (full IQ helpful). Personality. Social maturity. Alertness and drive.
Recording	*NB.* It is essential to record *separately*, the examiner's *clinical findings* and what is *reported* to him by others.
Conclusions and Recommendations	Developmental diagnosis. Recommendations for treatment, training and supervision.